Coconut's
Card Games

✪ American Girl™

Questions or comments? Call 1-800-845-0005,
visit our Web site at **americangirl.com,** or write to Customer Service,
American Girl, 8400 Fairway Place, Middleton, WI 53562-0497.

Printed in China
06 07 08 09 10 LEO 10 9 8 7 6 5 4 3 2

Coconut™, Licorice®, the Coconut and Licorice designs and logos,
and all American Girl marks are trademarks of American Girl, LLC.

Editorial Development: Sara Hunt

Art Direction: Camela Decaire, Chris David

Design: Camela Decaire

Production: Mindy Rappe, Kendra Schluter, Jeannette Bailey, Judith Lary

Illustrations: Casey Lukatz

Dear American girl,

This adorable deck of Coconut cards is sure to bring fun whenever and wherever you need a little something to do. Perfect for travel, sick days, or a day at the pool, these card games have been specially selected for American girls like you.

Try your hand at Coconut's card games—some are quick, some are loud. The enclosed book starts with games for one and ends with games for a crowd!

Your friends at American Girl

Contents

Need-to-Knows

Deal—to pass out cards to each player. Go around the circle to deal cards, one at a time, rather than giving four cards (or however many) at a time to each player.

Dealer—the person who gets to shuffle and deal the cards. It's best to take turns being the dealer. To decide who goes first, have everyone draw a card. The player who draws the highest card is the first to deal.

Discard—to get rid of a card from your hand. The discard pile is the pile where you put cards that you don't want.

Draw—to take a card. The draw pile is the pile that you take a card from.

Hand—the cards that are dealt to you. If your hand gets particularly hard to hold, sometimes you can set it up under a table or in a spot no one can see while you play.

Rank—refers to the number or face on the card (3s, jacks, and aces are all ranks).

Shuffle—when playing cards, it's important to mix up the cards in between each game or round. To shuffle your Coconut cards, you might cut the deck.

Suit—refers to the symbol on the card (hearts, clubs, spades, and diamonds are the four suits).

No peeking! Card games are more fun if you don't know what cards the other players have. So keep your cards from peering eyes and try to avoid the temptation yourself to peek at others' cards!

Beat
the
Clock

Goal Place all the cards around the clock.

Setup

Deal out all cards facedown into 13 piles of four cards each. Place 12 piles in a circle so that each pile represents a number on a clock. Create the 13th pile in the middle of the circle.

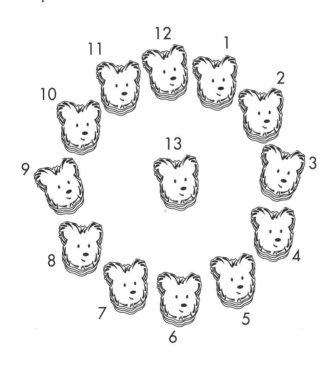

How to play Beat the Clock

1. Turn over the top card of the 13th pile and slip it, faceup, under the pile where its number would be on the clock. (For example, if it's a 2, slip it under the pile of cards in the 2 o'clock position.) A jack is 11, a queen is 12, a king is 13 (the middle pile), and an ace is 1.

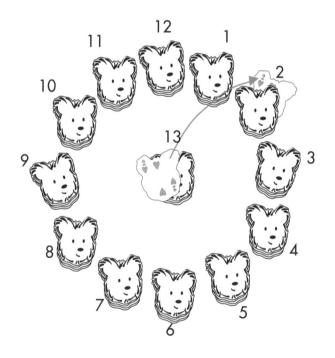

2. Then turn over the top card on *that* pile.

3. Slip the new card under the pile where its number is on the clock.

4. Continue turning over cards and placing them around the clock.

5. If all cards are turned faceup before the 4th king, you win!

Flower Garden

Goal Fill each basket with flowers from the garden.

Setup

1. Make 8 flowers, or fans, of faceup cards with 3 cards each. This is the *flower garden*.

2. Leave room above the flower garden to place the 4 aces in a row. These will be the *baskets*.

3. From your deck, turn over 3 cards and line them up in a row. These are the *seed cards*.

Baskets

Flower Garden

Seed Cards

How to play Flower Garden

1. You can only move cards that are on top of the flowers or seed piles.

2. Move free aces above the flower garden to start the baskets.

3. Build the baskets with cards in ascending number order—don't worry about the suit. For example, ace, 2, 3, 4, and so on until you get to a king.

4. Once you've moved all the cards you can into the baskets, turn over three more seed cards in the seed piles. You may move the top card only onto another flower in the garden in descending number order (10, 9, 8, 7, etc.) to get to a card below.

5. Shuffle and reuse the seed cards until the baskets are filled or you can't make any more moves.

> You don't HAVE to move a card.
> So think about it before you do!

Goal Round up all the cards in the deck to win.

How to play Animal Talk

1. Each player picks an animal and tells the other players what it is. The dealer deals out all the cards in the deck. Don't look at your hand.

2. Players keep their cards in a pile facedown in front of them. On the count of 3, each player turns her top card faceup on the table.

3. Players keep turning over cards at the same time as fast as they can, until 2 players flip over two cards that match. When that happens, the players who turned over the matching cards each make the other's animal sound. The player who makes the correct sound first takes the other player's faceup cards and adds them to the bottom of her pile.

4. If both players make the correct sound at the same time, no one gets the cards. If a player makes the wrong sound or makes a sound when there's no match, she gives her faceup cards to the other player. If there's a dispute over who made the right sound first, the other players make the call.

5. If you run out of cards to turn over, don't worry! You can re-enter play if someone turns over a card that matches your top card. Just be the first to make the other player's sound and you take the cards.

6. The game ends when one player has all the cards or only one player has cards left to play. She is the winner.

Pick a different animal for each new game to make it tricky!

Cat 'n' Mouse

Goal Collect all the cards.

How to play Cat 'n' Mouse

1. The dealer deals out all the cards. Each player keeps her pile facedown in front of her. No peeking!

2. The player to the dealer's left quickly turns over her first card and places it in the center.

3. The next player quickly follows, placing her card on top of the first player's card in the center, and so on until someone turns over an ace or a face card (a jack, queen, or king).

4. The girl who put down the ace or face card can take the stack of cards, BUT FIRST . . .

The player to her left gets a chance to take the stack by turning over cards and seeing if she gets an ace or a face card herself. The number of cards she can turn over is based on the card that was played.

Ace = 4 cards   Queen = 2 cards
King = 3 cards   Jack = 1 card

19

5. If the second player does not turn over an ace or a face card, the girl who originally put down the ace or face card takes the stack, adds the cards to the bottom of her pile, and starts a new round by laying down a card.

6. If the second player does turn over an ace or a face card, she gets the stack, BUT FIRST . . .

The player to *her* left gets a chance to take it (by following the same process outlined in step 4), and so on until someone wins the stack outright.

The player who collects all the cards wins!

Once you get the hang of it, play that whenever 2-of-a-kind are turned over consecutively, the first player to slap the pile gets to take the stack. Players who run out of cards can re-enter the game by slapping 2-of-a-kind.

Crazy Cards

Goal Get rid of all your cards. Eights are wild.

Setup

The dealer shuffles the cards and deals 5 cards facedown, one at a time, to each player. Place the rest of the deck facedown in a stack in the center of the playing area. This is the draw pile.

Turn over the top card from the draw pile and place it beside the pile, faceup. This is the discard pile. If the top card is a wild card, bury it in the draw pile and turn over the next card.

It helps to arrange the cards in your hand by suit and rank.

How to play Crazy Cards

1. Play starts with the player on the dealer's left. She plays a card that matches the top card—either its suit or its number. For example, if the card is the 9 of hearts, she can play any heart card or another 9.

2. If a player can't match suit or rank, she may play a wild card, if she has one. A wild card can stand for any suit you choose, but you must name a suit when you play a wild card.

3. If a player can't match suit or rank, and she doesn't have a wild card, she must draw a card from the draw pile. If she can use it, she may play it; otherwise her turn is over.

4. Play continues around the circle, with each player trying to match the last card played. The first girl to get rid of all her cards wins.

Note: To play Crazy Cards with 2 players, deal 7 cards each instead of 5.

Mini Golf

Goal Have the lowest-value hand at the end of the round. Play 9 holes or 18—each deal equals one hole.

Cards are worth their face value, except:

Ace = 1 point	Queen = 10 points
King = 0 points	Jack = 10 points

Setup

The dealer deals 4 cards, one at a time, to each player. Each player arranges her cards facedown in a square like this:

Place the rest of the cards facedown in a pile in the center of the playing area. This is the draw pile. Take the top card and place it faceup beside the draw pile to start the discard pile.

Each player looks—once—at the two bottom cards in her square layout, without showing them to any other players.

How to play Mini Golf

1. On your turn, either take the first card on the draw pile or the top card on the discard pile. If you pick up the card from the discard pile, you must use it and place one of the cards from your square on the discard pile.

2. You can either use the card you draw to replace one of the four cards in your square, or you can discard it. *You cannot look at your cards again before you decide.*

3. If you choose to keep the card you drew, place the card it replaced faceup on the discard pile.

4. If you do not want to use the card you drew, place it faceup on the discard pile.

Winning

1. If you think you have the lowest score, use your turn to knock on the table instead of drawing a card.

2. Each other player may take one more turn (to draw from the draw or discard piles but not to knock). Then play ends and everyone turns over her cards.

3. Total the value of the cards in each player's square based on the point values on page 25.

4. The player with the lowest score wins the hole. Total your scores for 9 holes to see who wins the round!

Go
Fetch!

Goal To collect all 4 cards of the same rank.

Setup

The dealer deals 5 cards to each player. The remaining cards are placed facedown in a draw pile. The player to the dealer's left begins play.

How to play Go Fetch!

1. On your turn, ask another player for a specific card rank: "Jenna, do you have any 4s?" You must have in your hand at least one of the rank cards you request. Jenna must give you all the 4s she has. If you receive the card you asked for, you go again and ask any player for any rank (as long as you have a card of that rank).

2. If Jenna does not have any 4s, she says, "Go fetch!" You then draw the top card from the draw pile. If the card you draw matches the rank you asked for, you show it and go again. If the drawn card is not the rank you asked for, you keep it, but your turn is over.

3. It's now Jenna's turn. The last player who is asked for a card gets to go next.

Winning

1. When you have all 4 of a particular rank, place the set faceup in front of you.

2. Play continues until one player is out of cards or the draw pile is used up. The winner is the player with the most sets of 4 at the end of play.

Note: To play Go Fetch! with 2 players, deal 7 cards each instead of 5.

Young Pup

#1 Young Pup

Goal Match your cards and get the "Young Pup."

Setup

Remove one jack from the Coconut deck. Set it aside. The dealer deals out all the cards, one at a time, to the players. It does not matter if one person has more cards.

How to play Young Pup

1. Players look at their cards and discard any pairs they have. A pair is 2 cards of equal rank (such as two 3s or two queens).

2. The dealer goes first. On her turn, she holds her hand out (facedown) to the player on her left. That player picks a card from the dealer's hand without peeking and adds it to her hand. If it makes a pair in her hand, she may discard the pair.

3. The player who just took a card then offers her hand to the player on her left, and so on.

To end the game

Continue play until all cards are used up. Eventually one player will be left with an unmatched jack (the Young Pup) and that player wins. All the remaining players call out "Young Pup!" and the game is over.

Dog-Gone

Goal Collect 4-of-a-kind and put your finger on your nose. Once someone has her finger on her nose, make sure you do, too!

Setup

The dealer shuffles the cards and deals 4 cards to each player. She puts the rest of the cards in a pile, facedown, in front of her. Players pick up their cards and arrange their hands.

How to play Dog-Gone

1. To begin, the dealer draws a card from the pile. She determines if she wants to keep the card to replace any of the cards in her hand. (Remember, the goal is to get 4-of-a-kind.)

2. If she wants to keep the drawn card, she discards a different card from her hand, facedown on the playing surface, to the player on her left. If she doesn't want to keep the drawn card, she discards it facedown to the player on her left.

3. On "go," players pick up a card from the player on their right and keep it or pass it facedown to the player on their left.

4. Girls should keep passing unwanted cards to their left and picking up cards from the right as fast as they can.

5. If you get 4-of-a-kind, stop passing cards and silently touch one finger to the tip of your nose.

6. If you see another player touch her nose, quickly and quietly touch your own nose. The last girl to touch her nose gets a "D."

7. Collect all the cards, shuffle, deal, and begin the game again. When someone loses for a second time, she gets the letter "O"; on the third time, she gets a letter "G." When she has "D-O-G," she has to say "Woof!" 3 times, and she's out.

Winning
The last girl left in the game without getting "D-O-G" wins.

Goal Be the first to bluff all your cards away.

Setup

The dealer shuffles the deck and deals all the cards. Players sort their cards by rank, creating a pile with the lowest on top. Hold your cards.

How to play No Way!

1. The player to the dealer's left goes first. She has to start with 2s. As she lays down her "2s" in a neat stack, facedown, she calls out what she's playing. For example, she says, "three 2s."

2. Now the other players must decide whether or not they think she's bluffing.

   Hint: Look at your cards. If you already have two 2s in your hand, it's impossible for her to have three 2s.

3. If a girl thinks the first player is bluffing, she challenges her by yelling "No way!" Then the first player has to turn her cards faceup. (If two girls

yell "No way!" at the same time, the girl closest to the player's left is the challenger.)

4. If the player was telling the truth, the challenger has to take the cards. If she was bluffing, she has to take her cards back. Her turn is over.

5. If no one challenges the first player, the cards stay facedown on the table. The next player who loses a challenge has to take all the cards on the table.

6. The game continues in the same way. The next player lays down 3s, the player after her lays down 4s, and so on. After the aces, start with 2s again.

7. The first player to get rid of all her cards wins!

To master the fine art of bluffing, you have to make other players think you're fibbing when you're not . . . and think you *aren't* when you are!

Coconut's Rummy

Goal Get rid of all your cards by collecting as many 3-of-a-kinds or runs as you can.

Setup

The dealer shuffles the deck and deals 7 cards to each player. Place the deck facedown in the center of the table. This is the draw pile. Turn the first card faceup and place it next to the pile. This will be the discard pile.

Each player looks at her hand for 3- or 4-of-a-kind, or a run—3 or more cards of the same suit in numerical order (for example, 6, 7, and 8 of spades). The ace can be used as a high card or a low card.

How to play Coconut's Rummy

1. The player to the dealer's left begins the game. If she can use the top card on the discard pile, she may pick it up and add it to her hand.

2. If the player cannot use the top card, she picks up a card from the draw pile. She may keep it or discard it. Any time a player has 3-of-a-kind or a run, she lays those cards down in front of her.

3. On her turn, a player can also add to another player's run or 3-of-a-kind by laying a card down on the table in front of her. For example, she can lay down a 7 to add to another player's 7, 7, and 7, or she can lay down a 2 of diamonds to add to another player's run of 3, 4, and 5 of diamonds.

4. At the end of her turn, the player must take one card from her hand and put it faceup on the discard pile.

5. If all of the cards in the draw pile are used before the game is over, start a new pile by shuffling the discard pile.

6. When one player uses all her cards, she yells "Rummy!"

Scoring

To get the winner's score, add up the cards in the other players' hands:

> Number cards = face value
>
> Face cards = 10 points each
>
> Aces = 15 points

Winning

The first player to reach 250 points wins. For longer games, play to 500; for shorter games, play to 100.

Note: You can also play the game so that players can take a card that is not on top of the discard pile— along with every card on top of it. For instance, if you want the 2 here, you need to take the ace, 10, and 4, too.

1-2-3 Stop!

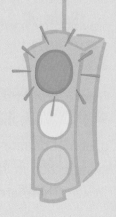

Goal Get rid of your cards—and win M&M's by playing pay cards!

Getting started

From a standard deck of cards (not the Coconut card deck), remove the ace of hearts, the king of clubs, the queen of diamonds, and the jack of spades. Place them faceup in the center of the playing area as shown. These are the *pay cards*.

Each player receives about 20 M&M's® (or Skittles®, beads, buttons, or other small objects). Players "pay up" by placing 1 M&M on each of the 4 pay cards. The dealer places 2 M&M's on each card.

Setup

The dealer shuffles and deals all the Coconut cards, beginning at her left and going around, including one extra hand for an imaginary player—Coconut!— on her immediate right. Don't worry if some players have more cards.

After looking at her hand, the dealer may decide to play Coconut's hand instead. She can look at her hand, but she cannot peek at Coconut's hand before deciding.

If the dealer keeps her own hand, the other players can bid against each other for Coconut's hand—the highest bidder wins, and the winner adds M&M's equal to her bid to the pay-card piles (distributed evenly among the 4 pay cards).

> Before play starts, it's helpful to sort your cards first by suit, then from lowest to highest within each suit. If it's hard to hold so many cards, create four piles in front of you (one for each suit). Whenever a specific suit is being played, just pick up that pile.

How to play 1-2-3 Stop!

1. The player to the dealer's left goes first. She may choose any suit in her hand, but she must put down the smallest card she has in the suit. (Aces are high for this game.)

2. The girl who has the next highest card in that suit then plays it, followed by the girl with the next highest card, and so on. Play does not necessarily go in a circle but jumps around depending on who has the next highest card. Play continues until the ace is played or, if the ace isn't available, until the highest card available is played. Then play "stops."

   Note: If you have consecutive cards in the same suit, you should play them all at once (for example, the 3 of hearts, 4 of hearts, and 5 of hearts).

3. The player who had the highest card available when play "stopped" selects the next suit, starting with the lowest available card in her hand.

4. Repeat steps 2 and 3, playing the next highest card in the suit each time until the ace is played or no higher card is available and all suits are played (or there's a winner).

Winning

The first player to discard all of her cards wins. The remaining players must "pay" the winner 1 M&M for each card remaining in their hands.

Winning the payout piles

When a player plays a card that matches one of the pay cards (the ace of hearts, the king of clubs, the queen of diamonds, or the jack of spades), she gets to collect all of the M&M's piled on that card. Everybody else starts the pile over by adding 1 M&M each.

> Pay cards aren't cleared during every game, so just keep piling up the M&M's for a big payout in a later game.